Bosses & Other Reptiles

RODD ZOLKOS

CONTEMPORARY
BOOKS

CHICAGO

Library of Congress
Cataloging-in-Publication Data

Bosses and other reptiles / [compiled by]
Rodd Zolkos.
     p.   cm.
   ISBN 0-8092-3617-6
    1. Supervisors—Quotations,
  maxims, etc.   2. Supervisors—
  Humor.   I. Zolkos, Rodd.
  PN6084.S84B67   1994
  658—dc20   94-22502
                         CIP

Published by Contemporary Books, Inc.
Two Prudential Plaza, Chicago, Illinois
  60601-6790
Manufactured in the United States
  of America
International Standard Book Number:
  0-8092-3617-6
10   9   8   7   6   5   4   3   2   1

For Kathy,
who put me up to this
in the first place

ACKNOWLEDGMENTS

. . . .

Thanks to the bosses of the world, without whom this book would not have been possible.

INTRODUCTION

. . . .

Chief. The Queen. The Big Heat. King Jerk. He or she is called by many names, and only the luckiest among us have never had to deal with one of his kind. He's The Boss.

Not that all bosses are bad. Many can be mentors, educators, counselors, friends—people who give us that boost we need as we make our way up the career ladder. A brush with a boss of that sort is an experience to be treasured the rest of your working life.

But what is it that really gives that kind of boss experience its value? That's right: all the rest of the bosses in the world. The teeming masses of management yearning to breathe incompetent. If you've worked for one, you know it. If you're working for one, God help you.

These are the sadists and the shallow, the insecure and the inconsistent, who send you home at the end of the day ready to howl from rage and frustration. Howl, that is, if you've got the strength left after a day of not just doing your job but trying to deal with someone who holds your life cupped in his or her hand eight hours a day, five days a week, fifty-two weeks a year (minus vacation). If you didn't know better, you would swear that person was hired solely because the folks at the top of the company food chain had somehow determined that there's long-range corporate benefit to be had by turning the workplace into your own personal living Hell.

Why do you think they call it "work," anyway? According to definition 1a in the tenth edition of *Merriam Webster's Collegiate Dictionary*, work is "sustained physical or mental effort to over come obstacles and achieve an objective or result." If *boss* has become synonymous with *obstacle* in your mental thesaurus, then your everyday objective isn't what you can achieve on the job but just survival. At that point it's not a question of whether you can grow professionally on the job but whether you can get out with some semblance of sanity. Have a nice day. Lotto, anyone?

You say yours is the good fortune never to have worked for one of these bosses? C'mon. Even Superman had Perry White. Okay, so Superman was mild-mannered Clark Kent then, but you get the point. And even if you *really* believe you have never had a bad boss, can you honestly claim never to have yearned, even for the briefest moment, for the chance to utter the timeless words of Johnny Paycheck: "Take this job and shove it"?

So, truth be told, we've all been there. But don't look at it as oppression of the many by the few but rather as a great unifying experience that binds us together each time one of us swallows hard and says, "I'll get right on that, boss." It's an experience we all share, and one that those quoted in these pages have, with varying degrees of eloquence, found words to describe in examining these "bosses and other reptiles."

Crazy bosses have a long and noble tradition. Consider Pharaoh giving Moses that terrible performance review. Everybody has stories about someone who was really nice before he became a boss and then turned into a raving, anxiety-laden paranoid wimp. While not at all useful in private life, these deficiencies often are uniquely suited to a successful business career.

—*Stanley Bing,* Newsweek

When a man tells you that he got rich through hard work, ask him *whose?*

—*Don Marquis*

I worked with a fire chief who resented demands by male firefighters that hazing rituals stop and complaints by female firefighters of sexual harassment and discrimination. He said they were all wimps.

—*Laree Kiely, assistant professor of business communication, University of Southern California*

The desire of one man to live on the fruits of another's labor is the original sin of the world.

—*James O'Brien, Irish Chartist leader*

We asked managers who had been in the job for only a few weeks or months to describe what it meant to be a manager. Nearly all of them began by discussing the rights and privileges of management, not its duties. They spoke of having total authority, being in charge, calling the shots. While they saw themselves as agenda-setters and decision-makers, these actions and decisions that they focused on dealt primarily with sales and business matters, seldom with people.

—*Linda Hill, associate professor, Harvard Business School,* Black Enterprise

The world is full of willing people; some willing to work, the rest willing to let them.
—*Robert Frost*

We are talking here, about a man who ran the whole Philippine islands for twenty-six years like it was some kind of personal dog kennel. He used silk handkerchiefs like Kleenex and routinely stole 10,000 full-grown mahogany trees with a single telephone call.
—*Hunter S. Thompson, on Ferdinand Marcos,* Generation of Swine

It is hard to look up to a leader who keeps his ear to the ground.
—*James H. Boren*

Some of the biggest bores I've ever known are men who have been highly successful in business, particularly self-made heads of big companies. Before the first olive has settled into the first martini, they pour the stories of their lives into the nearest and sometimes the remotest ears capturable.
—*Malcolm Forbes*

There is no necessary connection between the desire to lead and the ability to lead, and even less to the ability to lead somewhere that will be to the advantage of the led.

—*Bergen Evans,* The Spoor of
  Spooks and Other Nonsense,
  1954

Boss: This is the end. You're fired!
Worker: Fired? I always thought
  that slaves were sold.
—*Myron Cohen*

Normal is . . . sitting at a desk all day, under artificial light, eating machine food, hemmed in by four walls, with a plastic plant, a telephone, a Rolodex, a sense of déjà vu and a manager who says you better start "thinking outside the envelope."

—*Ellen Goodman*

Wages is a cunning device of the devil, for the benefit of tender consciences, who would retain all the advantages of the slave system, without the expense, trouble and odium of being slave-holders.

—*Orestes A. Brownson,*
The Boston Quarterly
Review, *1840*

It's all because I didn't recognize the big boss's voice over the phone from New York. He told me that if I asked him what his name was again, he'd fire me—and he did.

—*former receptionist, quoted in the* Chicago Tribune

We live under a system where many are exploited by the few, and war is the ultimate sanction of that exploitation.

—*Harold J. Laski, English political scientist, 1945*

The fellow who never makes mistakes takes his orders from one who does.
—*Herbert V. Prochnow*

Let the officers and directors of our armament factories, our gun builders and munitions makers and shipbuilders all be conscripted—to get $30 a month, the same wage paid to the lads in the trenches. Give capital thirty days to think it over and you will learn by that time there will be no war. That will stop the racket—that, and nothing else.
—*Smedley Butler, U.S. Marine commander, 1934*

I'm no fool. I've killed the boss.
You think they're not going to
fire me for a thing like that?
—*Lily Tomlin, as Violet
Newstead, in* 9 to 5

Maybe the boss can force a person to show up for work, especially in trying economic times;
but one cannot, by definition,
force a person to contribute her
or his passion and imagination
on a regular basis.
—*Tom Peters*

The workingmen have been exploited all the way up and down the line by employers, landlords, everybody.

—*Henry Ford*

Most workers know who the good bosses are—and, of course, who the bad ones are. Just ask.

—*Ann Therese Palmer,*
Chicago Tribune

We'd hear the yelling and say to ourselves, "There's another poor bastard getting his guts eviscerated."

> —*former Hill Holliday employee, describing CEO John Connors*

When asked if they had ever been fired, nearly one-third of the class members said they had. Not "resigned," not "down-sized"—"fired."

> —*Dale Dauten, "The Corporate Curmudgeon" columnist, referring to a Harvard Business School fifteen-year class reunion*

QUESTION: How many corporate vice-presidents does it take to screw in a light bulb?
ANSWER: Two. One to screw it in. One to screw it up.
—*Suds Lonigan,*
Funny Business

A corporation prefers to offer a job to a man who already has one, or doesn't immediately need one. The company accepts you if you are already accepted. To obtain entry into paradise, in terms of employment, you should be in a full state of grace.
—*Alan Harrington,*
Life in the Crystal Palace

She was forced to put on blouses with bows, blazers with crisp collars and gobs of foundation to narrow what her bosses considered a jutting chin.

—journalist Jane Gross, on former television news anchor Christine Craft, who was fired for being too old, too ugly, and not deferential to men

I've met a few people in my time who were enthusiastic about hard work. And it was just my luck that all of them happened to be men I was working for at the time.

—Bill Gold

Reagan liked his style and gave him all the room he needed—not just for hiring and firing and whipping his enemies with career-crushing "administrative punishments" that permanently destroyed anybody he didn't like; in addition to that, he was given a ranking advisory role that he rode all the way into the White House.

—*Hunter S. Thompson, on Ed Meese,* Generation of Swine

I can hire one half of the working class to kill the other half.

—*Jay Gould, nineteenth-century American capitalist*

Some 40 percent of those polled have experienced the joys of downsizing, nearly 30 percent have witnessed some management cuts, [and] 20 percent worry about being fired.
—*David Warsh*, Boston Globe, *on a 1993 survey of American workers*

I'm not going to be able to work for this f***ing beer nut.
—*Garry Shandling, as Larry, on brewery owner and potential network buyer Richard Germaine, on* The Larry Sanders Show

A ROSE BY ANY OTHER NAME
PART I

He prefers to refer to himself as Ming the Merciless, after a comic-book villain.
>   —*Christine Dugas, on corporate turnaround expert Sanford C. Sigoloff*

. . . .

Every time I went to see Jack I'd ask his secretary, "Who am I going to see today, Jack or Bob?" Bob was what we called his dark side.
>   —*former Hill Holliday manager, on CEO John Connors*

. . . .

The thing you have to under-stand about John is that he's a

nerd and he's always been a nerd.

—*John Sculley's wife, Leezy, describing the former Apple Computer CEO*

Harry is a complete idiot. He forgets what he tells you. He changes his mind about what he wants you to do and how to do it. Since we work for a major airline, when Harry screws up, the results are disastrous.

—Bosses from Hell: True Tales from the Trenches, *by Matthew Sartwell*

"Oh, Dixon, can I have a word with you?"

To its recipient this was the most dreadful of all summonses. It had been a favorite of his flight-sergeant's, a Regular with old-fashioned ideas about the propriety of getting an N.C.O. out of the men's hearing before subjecting him, not to a word, but to an uproar of abuse and threats about some harmless oversight.

—*Kingsley Amis,* Lucky Jim

I dread every holiday. . . . My husband's boss and his wife always go away and ask my husband and me to take care of

their house, garden, dogs and plants.
—*writer to Ann Landers*

What we've gotten at long last is an admission, after ten years, that they did something wrong.
—*attorney Frank Parkerson, on two management officials' admission of reckless behavior in allowing a manufacturing firm employee to be exposed to cyanide while working. By pleading guilty to involuntary manslaughter, the employers avoided a retrial on a charge of murder for the employee's subsequent death.*

This guy is a genius—but then, so was Al Capone. He's the smartest guy you'll ever meet. He's brilliant. But he stands for nothing, and has contempt for anyone that walks and talks.

—*Paramount CEO Martin S. Davis, on cable television magnate John C. Malone*

The American system of ours, call it Americanism, call it Capitalism, call it what you like, gives each and every one of us a great opportunity if we only seize it with both hands and make the most of it.

—*Al Capone*

The economy has made crazy bosses even crazier. With the tremendous anxiety that entered the workplace in the 1980s and 1990s, we have a festering hot-house of dysfunction that breeds crazy bosses.

—*Stanley Bing*

Our boss was so bad to everyone that on the day of his retirement, one of our group went to the laboratory and had a vial of blood drawn. At the party for his retirement we gave him the vial, saying, "You always wanted the last drop of our blood—here it is."

—*an entry in the*
Miller Business Systems'
"Bad Boss" contest

It comes down to not just one odd, sick or personality-disordered person. It is usually a situation in which there are persons at higher levels who unwittingly foster that.

> —*Leonard Speery, a psychiatric consultant to several Fortune 500 corporations*

Strategies are okayed in boardrooms that even a child would say are bound to fail. The trouble is, there is never a child in the boardroom.

> —*Victor Palmieri, business turnaround boss*

So much of what we call management consists of making it difficult for people to work.

—*Peter Drucker*

Some Arizona government offices were charging their employees 5 cents for each personal copy made on a state copier. Taking into account employee time to submit payment and keep records of the transactions, I figured that collecting each nickel cost 70 cents.

—*Dale Dauten, "The Corporate Curmudgeon" columnist*

Performance is what matters most when you want to get ahead, but kissing up can make a real difference. People can be rewarded without it, but it won't be easy—and it won't be as often.

—*psychology professor Ron Deluga*

It never hurts to suck up to the boss.

—*the Ferengis' Thirty-Third Rule of Acquisition, cited by Quark on* Star Trek: Deep Space Nine

You are responsible for your own career. And part of that responsibility is dealing with your boss. I've seen careers end very quickly because a newly promoted employee became overly confident, thinking that hard work would be enough to see him through.

> —*management consultant Randolph W. Cameron,* Black Enterprise

Management is now where the medical profession was when it decided that working in a drug store was not sufficient training to become a doctor.

> —*Lawrence Appley,* Men at the Top, *1959*

The term *toady* itself dates back from the Middle Ages, when it was used to describe charlatans' flunkies who, in order to prove the curative powers of their bosses, would pretend to eat toads believed to be poisonous, then make "miraculous" recoveries.

Clearly, popping a toad into one's mouth, or even pretending to, was not a job for anyone with a normal ration of self-respect. Thus, the very first practitioners established the Toady Code: There is nothing, no matter how unappetizing or demeaning, a toady won't do to make the boss happy.

—*Owen Edwards,* Upward Mobility: How to Succeed in Business Without Losing Your Soul

The worst experience of my life. It was Japanese management theory on acid.

—*an ex-employee, on working for Harvey and Bob Weinstein of Miramax Films*

Half of the working class is slaving away to pile up riches of which they will be plundered by the upper class. The other half is plundering the plunderers.

—*George Bernard Shaw, On the Rocks*

Bosses are obsessed with problems and anything new looks like one. Your challenge is to make your ideas look like solutions.

—*Dale Dauten, "The*
   Corporate Curmudgeon"
   columnist

My son's immediate supervisor has demanded access to his private apartment anytime she wants.

—*writer to "Workplace*
   Solutions" column,
   Chicago Tribune

The more I move among workers and factories and other
plants, the stronger I become
convinced that it is advisable to
have as [a company] president a
practical man, preferably one
who has risen from the very bottom of the ladder. Workmen, I
find, have far more respect for
such men than for collar-and-
cuff executives knowing little or
nothing about the different
kinds of work which have to be
done by the workers. Wherever
circumstances call for placing a
financier or lawyer or papa's son
at the head of a large organization, he should be made chairman or some other title, but not
president.

—*B. C. Forbes*

No man goes before his time. Unless, of course, the boss leaves early.

—*Frances Merron*

The true influence of work in the crack-up of an executive comes down to this: a neurotic individual encounters in his work a special stress (or a series of stresses) that at some point unbearably intensifies the conflicts in his own personality; then he goes to pieces . . . though success can be the result of a strong neurotic drive, the neurosis will eventually make trouble for the individual.

—*Richard Austin Smith,*
Fortune, *1955*

There are an enormous number of managers who have retired on the job.

—*Peter Drucker*

As we view the achievements of aggregated capital, we discover the existence of trusts, combinations, and monopolies, while the citizen is struggling far in the rear or is trampled to death beneath an iron heel. Corporations, which should be the restrained creatures of the law and the servants of the people, are fast becoming the people's masters.

—*Grover Cleveland, 1888*

BOSSES' RULES TO LIVE BY
PART I

Don't steal; thou'lt never thus compete successfully in business. Cheat.

—*Ambrose Bierce*

. . . .

I like to engender a little friendly competition. A little brain matter on the walls never hurt anybody.

—*manager of a small textbook publisher quoting her boss,* Esquire

38

Seeing your job through rose-tinged glasses can be better for workers in some ways than the harsh light of reality.
> —*Barbara Ilargi,*
> *psychology professor,*
> *University of Rochester*

What do I care about the law. Hain't I got the power?
> —*Cornelius Vanderbilt,*
> *nineteenth-century*
> *American capitalist*

By the accident of fortune a man may rule the world for a time, but by virtue of love he may rule the world forever.

—*Lao-tzu*, The Simple Way, c. 565 B.C.

Management by terror is a time-honored technique because it works. The most mediocre men or women can suddenly seem dynamic, forceful, fearful—passing anxiety and hatred down the managerial pipe until they infect all who work under them.

—*Stanley Bing*, Esquire

People must understand what their jobs are, how their work fits in, how they could contribute. Why am I doing this? Whom do I depend on? Who depends on me? Very few people have the privilege to understand those things. Management does not tell them. The boss does not tell them. He does not know what *his* job is. . . . When people understand what their jobs are, then they make joy in their work. Otherwise, I think they cannot.

—*management guru*
W. Edwards Deming

The cult of power, the respect for the divine right of management, has throughout history produced the destruction of the system led in that manner. So it is today, where bully behavior is encouraged and rewarded in a wide range of business enterprises. The style itself is applauded in boardrooms and in the house organs of the business media as "tough," "no-nonsense," "hard as nails." When you see these code words, you know you're dealing with a bully boss and an organization on the verge of decline and eventual dissolution.

—*Stanley Bing,* Esquire

Tough is passé. Today you're
dealing with a variety of head
games. That's where the cruel-
ty is.
　—*Abraham Zaleznik,*
　　Harvard Business School

The habitually punctual make all
their mistakes right on time.
　—*Laurence Johnston Peter*

Workers in the U.S. . . . have
been treated like dog food for
the last 150 years.
　　　　—*Tom Peters*

WE CAN HARDLY WAIT

Only 41 percent of workers under thirty years are happy with their jobs, but that figure increases to 58 percent of those fifty to fifty-nine years old and 68 percent of those sixty to sixty-nine years old.

So, hang in there! The best, it seems, is yet to come.

—*Carol Kleiman, on the results of a public opinion survey,* Chicago Tribune

A relationship with a boss is like any other relationship. You have to decide whether or not it's worth the effort of making it

work. You're not put on this planet to get up and go to work for a total jerk.

—*Peter Wylie,* Problem Bosses: Who They Are and How to Deal with Them

I will do whatever the hell I want to do because I've had it with you and this trifling job. I don't need this shit, unlike you, Mr. Professional Ass Kisser.

—*Halle Berry, as Natalie, in* Strictly Business

If it's your boss doing the harassing, it's hard to tell him he's disgusting.
—*Sandra Weintraub, inventor of the Harasser Flasher, a battery-powered pin that can be made to flash red and make siren sounds when objectionable remarks are made*

This is a totally nonsmoking office for everyone else, but Josh owns it, so he gets to smoke. As I sit there, dying for a cigarette, he blows smoke in my face and says, "What's wrong, Janet? You look sick."
—*Bosses from Hell: True Tales from the Trenches, by Matthew Sartwell*

Managers often give muddled assignments and unclear directions not because they want to confuse their staffs (as some manipulative bosses might) but because they're too overwhelmed or too afraid to think through their plans. Similarly, they are excessively critical because they need to focus on their staffs' weaknesses in order to feel strong.

—*Adele Scheele,*
Working Woman

All kings is mostly rapscallions.
—*Mark Twain,*
The Adventures
of Huckleberry Finn

Stop crying. Go to the bathroom and throw up like a man.
—*Linda Fairstein, New York's chief sex-crimes prosecutor, on what she was told by her boss twenty years ago when he found her upset over the prospect of her first court summation*

Some bosses can be tough to work for because no matter what their employees say or do, or what the facts indicate should be done, the big guy must have it his way. Period.
—*Brian Dumaine*, Fortune

If the boss got it right in the first place, I wouldn't have to be going through all this.

—*employees' attitude about layoffs and downsizing, according to management consultant Craig Dreilinger*

All those memos and directives that you get from your boss and put into the recycling box eventually will come back as paper towels and toilet paper.

—*Michael Finn, owner of Recycling Services*

The kind of guy if you crossed him, he'd cut your balls off, but you wouldn't find out until tomorrow when you got them in the mail. I saw people ruined—pounded into dust.

—*a staffer of former New York governor Hugh Carey, on Robert Morgado, Carey's secretary*

Tyrants commonly cut off the stairs by which they climb unto their thrones.

—*Thomas Fuller (1608–1661)*, Worthies of England

"Now, gentlemen," the owner of a big dress house said as he looked around the conference table at his staff. "I have a suggestion to make about a change in company policy for the coming year." Smiling paternally at the men, he continued, "I'd like all your opinions, all of you. Those opposed to my little idea will signify by saying 'I resign.'"
—*Myron Cohen*

Crazy bosses don't get better, they get more crazy. They begin to show signs of strain, and, eventually, they blow up.
—*Stanley Bing*, Crazy Bosses: Spotting Them, Serving Them, Surviving Them

Tell Steve you can't do something because it violates the laws of physics, and he says that's not good enough.
—*a former Next Computer employee, on the unreasonable demands of Steven Jobs, one of seven CEOs chosen by* Fortune *as "America's toughest bosses"*

I'm nobody, but people shouldn't treat anyone like this.
—*artist Susan Davis, on being asked to work for six weeks for free to produce six versions of a presidential holiday card, all of which were rejected without comment*

He's definitely a few herbs short of the special recipe. He's touched in the head.

—New York Post *reporter Jim Nolan, on* Post *owner Abe Hirschfeld*

The businessman dealing with a large political question is really a painful sight. It does seem to me that businessmen, with a few exceptions, are worse when they come to deal with politics than men of any other class.

—*Henry Cabot Lodge, quoted by Arthur Schlesinger Jr., referring to Ross Perot's 1992 presidential bid*

It's hard to run a White House with nobody in charge. It's especially hard to run a White House with nobody in charge and two presidents.
—*an anonymous friend of the Clintons*

Now don't take this as a threat, but I killed a man like you in Korea, hand to hand.
—*Rip Torn, as producer Artie, to iron-willed network executive Melanie Parrish, on* The Larry Sanders Show

Bo knows who's boss. But that doesn't make it any easier when the boss tells him to sit.

—*Joey Reaves,*
Chicago Tribune

Frank Munsey, the great publisher, is dead.

Frank Munsey contributed to the journalism of his day the talent of a meat-packer, the morals of a money-changer, and the manners of an undertaker. He and his kind have about succeeded in transforming a once-noble profession into an 8 percent security. May he rest in trust.

—*William Allen White,*
editor, Emporia *(Kansas)*
Gazette, *1925*

It can be demeaning. It can be obvious. It can be juvenile. But "kissing up" to the boss still works; maybe that's why so many people do it.

    —*Mitchell Schnurman,*
       Fort Worth Star-Telegram

Some bosses are saying, "You better learn how to play golf or you're going to be left in the office."

    —*DeeDee Owens,*
       Cog Hill Golf Club pro

More knowledge may be gained of a man's real character by a short conversation with one of his servants than from a formal and studied narrative, begun with his pedigree and ended with his funeral.

—*Samuel Johnson,*
The Rambler

In the 1990s you get to keep your job for just as long as it takes your employer to export it, automate it or give it to one of your friend's children for half the money.

—*Martin Yate, author of*
Knock 'Em Dead:
The Ultimate Job
Seeker's Handbook

Many interviewers abuse and misunderstand the concept of being overqualified. Often, what it really means is that the applicant has more degrees and experience than the prospective boss.

—*Dr. Harry Levinson,*
  publisher of The Livens
  Letter, *which focuses on*
  the psychological aspects of
  leadership in organizations

No one can build his security upon the nobleness of another person.

—*Willa Cather,*
  Alexander's Bridge

Power is the great aphrodisiac.
—*Henry Kissinger*

For de little stealin' dey gits you in jail soon or late. For de big stealin' dey makes you emperor and puts you in de Hall o' Fame when you croaks. If dey's one thing I learns in ten years on de Pullman cars listenin' to de white quality talk, it's dat same fact.

—*Eugene O'Neill,*
The Emperor Jones

I cover crooks. I don't work for them.
  —New York Post *columnist Mike McAlary, on would-be* Post *owner and debt-collection magnate Steven Hoffenberg*

What is good for the country is good for General Motors, and what's good for General Motors is good for the country.
  —*Charles E. Wilson, American industrialist, in testimony to the Senate Armed Forces Committee, 1952*

As long as I count the votes, what are you going to do about it?
—*William Marcy "Boss" Tweed, 1871*

In downsizing, managers behave like people who know that someone is dying of a terminal illness. They don't know what to say, so they avoid the person [who's being laid off]. And because they don't know how to act, they pretend nothing's happening.
—*Andra Brooks, Ph.D., and Nicole Schapiro, industrial psychologist*

Wealth is power usurped by the few, to compel the many to labor for their benefit.
—*Percy Bysshe Shelley*

There will soon come an armed contest between capital and labor. They will oppose each other, not with words and arguments, but with shot and shell, gun-powder and cannon. The better classes are tired of the insane howling of the lower strata and they mean to stop them.
—*William Tecumseh Sherman, 1885*

The public be damned.
—*William H. Vanderbilt,*
  nineteenth-century
  American railroad
  president

It takes to support me just about twenty times as much as it takes to support an average working man or farmer. And the funny thing about it is that these working men and farmers work hard all year round, while I don't work at all.
—*Joseph Medill*
  Patterson, American
  newspaper publisher

When Bill asked for a sick day to care for their baby, his boss asked: "Why do you have to? That's what wives are for."

—from a 1993 report on work and family policies

I was a busybody asking, "Why aren't you doing it this way?" That doesn't sit well with authority. Bosses don't like a lot of questions.

—sculptor Ron Klowden, on his short-lived corporate career path

It probably wouldn't be a good career move to say, "Hey, John, what the hell is going on? I mean, you lend money to Brazil and Poland and I couldn't get a car loan. Energy firms? The Hunt brothers? Sure, *they're* a good risk."

—*middle manager at Manufacturers Hanover Trust Company, discussing the bank's problems and chairman John F. McGillicuddy in the late 1980s*

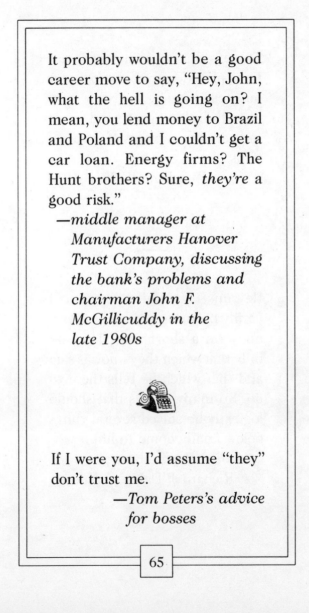

If I were you, I'd assume "they" don't trust me.

   —*Tom Peters's advice for bosses*

There was a time when corporations played a minor part in our business affairs, but now they play the chief part, and most men are the servants of corporations.

—*Woodrow Wilson, 1913*

He runs City Hall like a small family business and keeps everybody on a short rein. They do only that which they know is safe and that which he tells them to do. So many things that should logically be solved several rungs below finally come to him.

—*Mike Royko,* Boss: Richard J. Daley of Chicago

Management today does not know what its job is. In other words, [managers] don't understand their responsibilities. They don't know the potential of their positions. And if they did, they don't have the required knowledge or abilities. There's no substitute for knowledge.

— *management guru*
W. Edwards Deming

This is a small fragment of the glass ceiling. Women are being told by their boss to change their voice.

—*Keith G. Saxon,*
a physician who specializes
in vocal-cord problems

WHAT DO YOU HAVE
TO LOSE?

I asked the boss . . . whether he
thought my actions merited a
raise worth 15 cents per minute.
. . . He immediately agreed to
this minuscule incremental increase, not thinking at the time
that in an eight-hour workday,
this amounted to $9 an hour for
$72 a day—or $360 a week,
about $1,450 a month, to a total
of more than $17,000 a year!
Soon afterward, though, he did
the figuring and . . . admitted,
"You sure got me!"
   —*Nicole Schapiro, industrial
    psychologist and author of*
    Negotiating for Your Life:
    New Success Strategies
    for Women

If somebody . . . is told to work until she drops, then the boss really is saying, "We can replace you." It's time to look for another job.

    —*Debra Benton, author of* Lions Don't Need to Roar: How to Use Professional Presence to Stand Out

In our upside-down world, many business executives get more money if and when they lay off workers. The stock market and the unemployment rolls go up together.

    —*Ellen Goodman*

Our boss starts fights, screams obscenities and throws things over the smallest thing. We are concerned that she may hurt someone with that kind of temper.

—*writer to "Workplace Solutions" column,* Chicago Tribune

In this era of corporate downsizing, with companies slicing and dicing and cutting and chopping in an effort to reduce costs, it would appear that the only management tool a CEO needs is a well-honed VegaMatic.

—*Ronald E. Yates,* Chicago Tribune

The proletarians have nothing to lose but their chains. They have a world to win. Workers of the world, unite!

—*Karl Marx and Friedrich Engels,* The Communist Manifesto

The capitalist class is interested in keeping the workingmen divided among themselves. Hence it foments race and religious animosities that come down from the past.

—*Daniel DeLeon, American Socialist leader and writer, 1903*

Madame Boss . . . sticks her long, dirty fingernails into our salads and plucks out the olives. Yesterday she licked off her knife and stuck it into a container of cream cheese a co-worker had brought from home.

—*writer to Ann Landers*

If somebody could provide a vision, provide a sense of direction, we could make a lot more progress. [Then CEO] Roger Smith doesn't provide any inspiration at all for anybody.

—*a General Motors veteran*

Management has failed in this country. It is continuing to fail. It insists on ranking people with management-mandated performance criteria. . . . It leads to reward at the top and punishment at the bottom. It is a ruinous, chaotic system that removes joy from the workplace and leaves in its place mistrust and stress.

—management guru
W. Edwards Deming

In a hierarchy, every employee tends to rise to his level of incompetence.

—Laurence Johnston Peter,
The Peter Principle

I distinctly remember talking to the manager, who was sprawled out at his very large desk with his feet up on it, leaning back in his chair and his sleeves rolled up. He looked at me and said, "What are you using for birth control? How do we know you're not going to get pregnant?"

—*Deborah L. Flick, a lecturer in women's studies at the University of Colorado, referring to a 1971 interview for a marketing job*

The truth about the silly idea of top-down, authoritarian management . . . is that companies reap much more success by sow-

ing better working conditions and transferring as much responsibility and reward as possible to employees.
—*Stephen Franklin,*
Chicago Tribune

Most men would feel insulted if it were proposed to employ them in throwing stones over a wall, and then in throwing them back, merely that they might earn their wages. But many are no more worthily employed now.
—*Henry David Thoreau,*
Life Without Principle

Sick days . . . are made solely for rare diseases with names like phlebocysticmaxitosis. It's OK to call the office and say, "I won't be in today. I've got phlebocysticmaxitosis," but call and say "I've got a cold" and you may as well announce you're in Tahiti.
—*Mary Schmich,*
Chicago Tribune, *on the business world's notion that a cold is not a sickness but merely an inconvenience*

Bosses are like diapers: full of shit and always on your ass.
—*bumper sticker*

Oh, but he was a tightfisted hand at the grindstone. Scrooge! a squeezing, wrenching, grasping, scraping, clutching, covetous old sinner! Hard and sharp as flint, from which no steel had ever struck out generous fire; secret, and self-contained, and solitary as an oyster.

—*Charles Dickens,*
A Christmas Carol

Never burn bridges. Today's junior prick, tomorrow's senior partner.

—*Sigourney Weaver,*
as Katharine Parker,
in Working Girl

If there must always be a laboring population distinct from proprietors and employers, we regard the slave system as decidedly preferable to the system of wages.

—*Orestes A. Brownson,*
American writer and
founder of the Workingmen's
Party, 1840

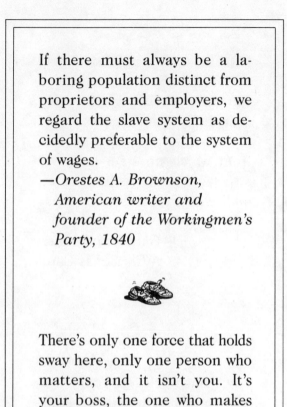

There's only one force that holds sway here, only one person who matters, and it isn't you. It's your boss, the one who makes Napoleon look like Gandhi, and you're trapped. There is no escape—only surrender.

—*Matthew Sartwell,*
Bosses from Hell: True Tales from the Trenches

"Do I detect the odor of liquor on your breath?" a stingy boss asked his sales manager.

"You do," admitted the sales manager. "I've just been celebrating the twentieth anniversary of the last raise you gave me."

—*Myron Cohen*

The gulf between employers and employed is constantly widening, and classes are rapidly forming, one comprising the very rich and powerful, while in another are found the toiling poor.

—*Grover Cleveland, 1888*

Each crazy boss mixes his or her own strange brew of odd behavior. He is a beautiful rainbow shading lightly from one hue of neurotic excess to the next. The crazy boss can have five faces: the vicious bully, the sniveling paranoid, the self-obsessed narcissist, the alternating fascist/wimp "bureaucrazy," and the chronic disaster hunter.

—*Stanley Bing,* Newsweek

He's been Sybilizing a lot lately with a lot of guys, not just me. You know, going through all the different personality stages—like Sybil, the girl in the movie.

—*former Chicago Bears quarterback Jim McMahon, on his coach, Mike Ditka*

WEIRDEST HABITS OF TERRIBLE SUPERVISORS:

- Clips nails with jumbo-size clipper during meetings
- Fills awkward silences by sucking food caught in his braces
- Imitates Mr. Magoo
- Moons employees, then denies it to his boss
- Rolls her eyes back until the whites show
- Wears souvenir Palestinian head-wrap at office
- Wrote *How Karate Made Me a Better Supervisor*
  —*responses to a request for "your boss's most unpleasant habit,"* Men's Health

Some executives are so crazed it's hard to imagine why anyone would work for them. Imagine a cross between Simon Legree and Captain Bligh, combined with the Joker, and you begin to grasp the idea: We're talking psycho bosses from hell.

—*Brian Dumaine*, Fortune

My boss had the habit of going through the employees' trash, looking for mistakes we had made. It got so bad that I used to tear up any mistakes and hide the bits in my shoes to be thrown out at home.

—*writer to Dear Abby*

I always thought I'd be a hotshot corporate secretary. I tried that. They sat me in a cubbyhole for eight hours a day, and I got in trouble when I laughed.

—*Coleen-Shannon "Chessie" Barrettsmith, who went on to manage the affairs of three companies and forty employees*

He liked to put people who didn't like each other together, tie up the bag, and let them claw it out.

—*a marketing specialist, on his boss's management style, "I Work for a Jerk,"* Men's Health

He seemed to suffer from that rare snobbery of the greedy rich, the attitude that suggests, "If you're so smart, how come you ain't rich like me?"

—Maureen Reagan,
on former White House
chief of staff Donald Regan

I'm calling about [Don] Regan's reaction to Bud. Did you hear it? Incredible. I have a source who swears to me that when Regan heard that Bud had attempted suicide and survived, Regan said, quote, That poor son of a bitch can't do anything right, unquote.

—what a reporter told Regan
speechwriter Peggy Noonan

following the attempted suicide by White House adviser Bud McFarlane, What I Saw at the Revolution

The work of the working people, and nothing else, produces the wealth, which, by some hocus-pocus arrangement, is transferred to me, leaving them bare. While they support me in splendid style, what do I do for them? Let the candid upholder of the present order answer, for I am not aware of doing anything for them.

> —*Joseph Medill Patterson, American newspaper publisher*

She said the idea was to "make your boss king for a day"—as if that title isn't part of the permanent job description.

—*Michael A. Levine,* Chicago Tribune, *on Patricia Haroski's 1958 creation of National Boss Day*

The Big Bad Boss is a destructive manager who has no respect for you, crushes your ego and on a daily basis whacks hard at your confidence.

—*Carol Kleiman,* Chicago Tribune

Another workplace myth may be shattered. Women do not appear to be noticeably more sympathetic as bosses than men, according to a national survey of 3,400 workers.
—*Mike Dorning,*
Chicago Tribune

You're eunuchs. How can your wives stand you? You've got nothing between your legs.
—*Warnaco CEO*
Linda Wachner, to several
of her male employees

My research shows that during a recession, bad bosses tend to get even more abusive because they think they can get away with it—employees are not going to quit or complain.

> —*Joseph R. Weintraub,*
> *management and*
> *organizational behavior*
> *professor, Babson College*

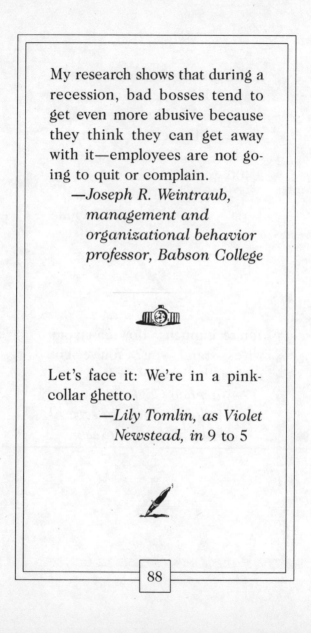

Let's face it: We're in a pink-collar ghetto.

> —*Lily Tomlin, as Violet*
> *Newstead, in* 9 to 5

He'd call you into the conference room, which everyone could see from the bull-pen area where we sat, and no matter what you'd done wrong, he'd always go over mistakes of the past. The guy never forgave you for anything, and there was no way you'd ever get a clean slate with him.

—*James B. Miller, author of* The Corporate Coach: How to Build a Team of Loyal Customers and Happy Employees, *on a former boss*

Robinson Crusoe started the forty-hour work week. He had all his work done by Friday.

—*Leopold Fechtner*

Labor, n.: one of the processes by which A acquires property for B.

—*Ambrose Bierce, 1911*

Bigness taxes the ability to manage intelligently. . . . The growth of bigness has resulted in ruthless sacrifices of human values. The disappearance of free enterprise has submerged the individual in the impersonal corporation. When a nation of shopkeepers is transformed into a nation of clerks, enormous spiritual sacrifices are made.

—*William O. Douglas, 1963*

Employees [were urged] to trim travel expenses by hitchhiking to business destinations, bunking with friends and ducking meal checks with the old dine-and-dash routine.

—Bloomberg Business News, *on a (joke) notice found on the bulletin board of Du Pont Company*

We are all controlled by the world in which we live, and part of that world has been and will be constructed by men. The question is this: are we to be controlled by accidents, by tyrants, or by ourselves in effective cultural design?

—*B. F. Skinner,* Cumulative Record, *1972*

Leadership is more likely to be assumed by the aggressive than by the able, and those who scramble to the top are more often motivated by their own inner torments than by any demand for their guidance.

—*Bergen Evans,*
  The Spoor of Spooks and
  Other Nonsense, *1954*

Don't look now, but your employer is spying on you. She's reading your e-mail, eavesdropping on your phone calls, counting your keystrokes, monitoring what's on your computer screen and tracking your whereabouts.

—*Cynthia Hanson,*
  Chicago Tribune

Many minor executives prefer a generous expense account to a raise in salary which would be heavily taxed and more soberly spent. It is they who support the so-called "expense-account restaurants," places of exotic décor where patrons lunch in the darkness which is all but complete. They cannot see to read the prices on the menu, but these, in the special circumstances, are irrelevant.

—*C. Northcote Parkinson*, The Law and the Profits, *1960*

My unemployed brother-in-law gave up his job because of illness. His boss got sick of him.

—*Henny Youngman*

Air safety depends on whether those in the cockpit can talk back to the boss. So does business survival.

—*Jim Kouzes*, Chicago Tribune

Big Brother is watching you.

        —*George Orwell*, 1984

The boss stood at the door, tapping his foot as Brokaw walked in.

"Brokaw, you should have been here at nine o'clock!"

"Why, what happened?"

        —*Suds Lonigan*,
        Funny Business

They come from all over the country to New York. The executive's wife decides they will move to New York. She says "John, you're the boss now. I've been doing the laundry and raising the kids all my life. It's time we enjoyed opening nights in New York." So the company packs up and moves to New York.
—*Webb & Knapp president*
  William Zeckendorf,
  predicting a continued
  New York office construction
  boom, 1959

He takes a perverse pleasure in seeing you twist in the wind.
        —*former Hill Holliday*
          manager, on CEO
          John Connors

A ROSE BY ANY OTHER NAME
PART II

General Electric Chairman Jack Welch has long been tagged "Neutron Jack" for his ability to eliminate thousands of people and still leave the buildings standing.
 —Bloomberg Business News

. . . .

If you look up the word *control freak* in the dictionary, there ought to be a picture of Jack right next to it.
—*a former colleague, on Hill Holliday CEO John Connors*

. . . .

Her nicknames, and that is speaking kindly, included "Steel Balls" and "Dawn of the Dead."
 —*Jessica Seigel,* Chicago

Tribune, on former Columbia Pictures president Dawn Steel

Do too many executives still indulge in the short-sighted habit of issuing orders without taking the slightest pains to explain to those responsible for carrying them out the whyfor and wherefor of the orders? Where employees come in daily and hourly contact with the public, surely it is important that care be taken to fit them to reply intelligently to courteous questions. "Because them are orders" isn't a very satisfactory reply—even less satisfactory to the management than to the public.

—*B. C. Forbes*

The history of all hitherto existing society is the history of class struggles. Freeman and slave, patrician and plebeian, lord and serf, guild master and journeyman, in a word, oppressor and oppressed, stood in constant opposition to each other, carried on an uninterrupted, now hidden, now open fight, a fight that each time ended, either in a revolutionary reconstruction of society at large, or in the common ruin of the contending classes.

—*Karl Marx and
   Friedrich Engels,*
   The Communist Manifesto

I have never seen anyone leap-frog so fast to the top in my life. And I have the bad back to prove it.

> —*Lily Tomlin, as Violet Newstead, in* 9 to 5, *on her boss*

The agencies of mass communication are big business, and their owners are big businessmen.

> —*Commission on Freedom of the Press, 1947*

The only compliments the boss should be paying female employees should involve their work and the compliment should be echoed in their paychecks.

—*Mary Schmich,*
Chicago Tribune

In the last analysis the property-owning class is loyal only to its own property.

—*John Reed (1887–1920),*
American journalist

We've all worked for bosses who insisted on rewrites to make things look better. With the computer, what you can expect becomes broad enough that you could spend forever, whereas with typewriters, there were limitations to what you could do.

—*Dan Schafer,*
   editor and publisher of
   Inventive Users Newsletter

[My boss] continued the conversation for twenty minutes, even though I alerted him each time a new contraction was beginning. My daughter was born an hour later. First thing the next morning guess who called my hospital to discuss business again?

—*a runner-up in the*
   Miller Business Systems'
   "Bad Boss" contest

The conflict in America is between two kinds of planning. It is privately planned scarcity by companies for profits or publicly planned economic abundance for people. This is really the struggle.
—*Walter P. Reuther,*
  American labor leader, 1952

Take this job and shove it.
          —*Johnny Paycheck*

Fascism is big business armed with bayonets.
          —*Grant Singleton,*
            American writer

Naziism along with Fascism is big business gone hydrophobia.

—*Oscar Ameringer, American writer and editor, 1942*

"So Martha, what kind of guy is your new boss?" asked a colleague on the elevator.

Martha rolled her eyes. "You know what boss is spelled backwards?

"Double S.O.B.!"

—*Suds Lonigan*
Funny Business

The employer puts his money into . . . business and the workman his life. The one has as much right as the other to regulate that business.

—*Clarence S. Darrow, 1909*

There is the instrument of our destruction. . . . He creates nothing, he builds nothing. And in his wake lies nothing but a blizzard of paper to cover the pain. Oh, if he said, "I know how to run your business better than you," that would be something worth talking about. But he's not saying that. He's saying, "I'm going to kill you, because at this particular moment in time you're worth more dead than alive."

—*Gregory Peck, as company president Andrew Jorgenson on Danny DeVito's "Larry the Liquidator" character, in* Other People's Money

I don't want any yes-men around me. I want everyone to tell the truth—even though it costs him his job.

—*Samuel Goldwyn*

Tess, Tess, Tess. You won't get ahead by calling your boss a pimp.

—*Olympia Dukakis,*
as the personnel director,
to Melanie Griffith, in
Working Girl

Why is it that employees, once lauded by CEOs as the most valuable asset of a company, are now considered liabilities or at best just another cost of production, to be whittled and squeezed and chopped and diced and discarded like some out-of-date mainframe computer or turret lathe?

—*Ronald E. Yates,*
Chicago Tribune

BOSSES' RULES TO LIVE BY
PART II

The typical big company executive believes that ancient bit of nonsense, "a rule is a rule."
—*Dale Dauten,*
"The Corporate
Curmudgeon" columnist

. . . .

You can't mine coal without machine guns.
—*Richard B. Mellon,*
American industrialist, 1937

. . . .

The way to have power is to take it.
—*attributed to William Marcy*
"Boss" Tweed

The fields were fruitful, and starving men moved on the roads. . . . The great companies did not know that the line between hunger and anger is a thin line.

—*John Steinbeck,*
The Grapes of Wrath

From that first institution of government to the present time there has been a struggle going on between capital and labor for a fair distribution of profits resulting from their joint capacities.

—*Martin Van Buren*

People are talking about the new "civilized" way to fire executives. You kick 'em upstairs. They're given a title, a liberal tithe, nothing to do, and a secretary to do it with. What a way to go!
— *Malcolm Forbes*

There never has yet existed a wealthy and civilized society in which one portion of the community did not, in point of fact, live on the labor of the other. Broad and general as is this assertion, it is fully borne out by history.
— *John C. Calhoun, 1837*

Guidelines for bureaucrats:
1. When in charge, ponder.
2. When in trouble, delegate.
3. When in doubt, mumble.
— *James H. Boren*

By treating the laborer first of all as a man, the employer will make him a better working man; by respecting his own moral dignity as a man, the laborer will compel the respect of his employer and of the community.
— *pastoral letter of the Catholic Archbishops of the United States, 1919*

The typical worker remains stoic when told there will be no raise, or possibly only a 2 percent increase. . . . Instead of licking your boss's hand gratefully and thanking the company for keeping you on the payroll even in these tough times, why not do what comes naturally? Burst into tears.

—*Carol Kleiman,*
Chicago Tribune

My boss Ed was very moody. He had a sign on his desk that said MY MOOD IS SUBJECT TO CHANGE AT A MOMENT'S NOTICE, like he was proud of his inconsistency.

—*a criminal attorney in a large urban firm, quoted in* Esquire

Every manufacturer ought to remember that his fortune was not achieved by himself alone, but by the cooperation of his workmen. He should acknowledge their rights to share the benefits of that which could not exist without their faithful performance of duty. Not until the capitalist is just enough to recognize this truth, can he ever join a group of workmen and feel himself among friends.

—*Peter Cooper,*
nineteenth-century
American industrialist

I have the most brilliant, generous and kindly boss—me.

—*John Slaven,*
Advertising Age

The capitalist class knows no country and no race, and any "God" suits it so that "God" approves of the exploitation of the worker.

—*Daniel DeLeon,*
American socialist leader
and writer, 1903

"Your salary is your personal business," a boss told his newest employee, "and it shouldn't be disclosed to anyone."

"I wouldn't think of mentioning it to anyone," came the reply. "I'm just as much ashamed of it as you are."

—*Myron Cohen*

The essence of all slavery consists in taking the produce of another's labor by force. It is immaterial whether this force be founded upon ownership of the slave or ownership of the money that he must get to live.

—*Leo Tolstoy*

QUESTION: Do you consider $10 a week enough for a long-shoreman with a family to support?

ANSWER: If that's all he can get, and he takes it, I should say it's enough.

—*J. Pierpoint Morgan,*
in testimony to the United
States Commission on
Industrial Relations

114

Just because an organization's needs aren't the same as what you can provide, it doesn't mean that you stink. In fact, it may be more true to say that *they* stink. How many stupid decisions did that company make in the last year, anyway?
  —*Stanley Bing,* Crazy Bosses:
    Spotting Them, Serving
    Them, Surviving Them,
    advising the recently fired

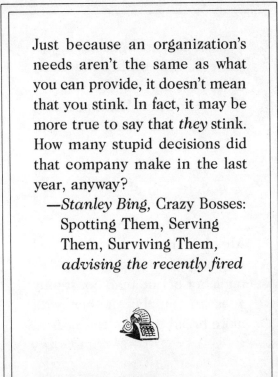

Hail, fellow, well met,
All dirty and wet;
Find out if you can,
Who's master, who's man.
  —*Jonathan Swift,*
    My Lady's Lamentation, *1765*

Capital has a right to a just share of the profits, but only to a just share.

—*Cardinal William Henry O'Connell, 1912*

All this life is senseless and tragic in which the endless slaving labor of one man constantly goes to supply another with more bread than he can use.

—*Maxim Gorky*

I remember my wonderment at a Time Inc. meeting some years ago when a fairly infamous corporate toady who had been complaining bitterly about the hopelessness of our fearless leader leapt to his feet when the boss entered the room, broke into a smile that was, frankly, terrible to behold, and exclaimed, "Hey, boss, *great* suit!"

—*Owen Edwards,*
Upward Mobility: How to
Succeed in Business Without
Losing Your Soul

As you know, employees always know more than their employers.

—*Franz Kafka,* The Trial

"Miss Frobish, you're late again," admonished her supervisor. "Is there any reason for this constant tardiness?"

"Yes, Mr. Rhodes. It makes the day shorter."

—*Suds Lonigan,*
Funny Business

From the moment one man began to stand in need of the help of another; from the moment it appeared advantageous to any one man to have enough provisions for two, equality disappeared, property was introduced, work became indispensable, and vast forests became smiling fields, which man had to water with the sweat of his brow,

and where slavery and misery were soon seen to germinate and grow up with the crops.
—*Jean-Jacques Rousseau,*
Origin of Inequality

Bosses from Hell are part of an ancient tradition. Remember Jacob? He worked for Laban for seven years to win the right to marry Rachel, then Laban tricked him into marrying her cross-eyed sister, Leah. So Jacob worked another seven years for Rachel, then six more just to get a decent severance package.
—*Matthew Sartwell,*
Bosses from Hell: True Tales from the Trenches

An institution is the lengthened shadow of one man.
—*Ralph Waldo Emerson*

Is not a patron, my lord, one who looks with unconcern on a man struggling for life in the water, and when he has reached ground encumbers him with help? The notice which you have been pleased to take of my labors, had it been early, has been kind; but it has been delayed till I am indifferent, and cannot enjoy it; till I am solitary, and cannot impart it; till I am known, and do not want it.
—*Samuel Johnson, in a letter to Lord Chesterfield*

A leader is best
When people barely know he
　exists.
Not so good when people obey
　and acclaim him,
Worse when they despise him.
"Fail to honor people,
They fail to honor you";
But of a good leader, who talks
　little,
When his work is done, his aim
　fulfilled,
They will say, "We did this
　ourselves."
　　　　　—*Lao-tzu, c. 565 B.C.*

Remember the basic tenet of all crazy-boss relations: He can own your soul only if you give it to him. Don't.

—*Stanley Bing*, Esquire